Betcha Don't Know *Jack* About Libertarianism

by
Kenneth DeLong

First Edition, 2018

ISBN-10: 1719490872
ISBN-13: 978-1719490870

Acknowledgements

The author would like to thank Cleo Lepart for her work in reviewing and editing the manuscript, as well as my daughters Erin and Olivia for helping with the cover concept.

I would also like to thank Ron Paul, Dave Smith, and Jason Stapleton for helping me to understand, and Murray Rothbard, for helping us all to understand.

Table of Contents

Introduction

Ah, modern politics. Team Red attacks Team Blue. Team Blue attacks Team Red. Whichever team gets power can't wait to put the hurt on the other team. Tribalism at its ugliest. It's all so disheartening, but what alternative do we have?

I mean, there are the libertarians, of course. But everyone knows they are crazy. I'm not quite sure what their positions are, but I read in the press that they are definitely not reasonable.

Crazy, unreasonable? Indeed, many conclusions of libertarianism may sound odd, surprising, even crazy, at first. But there's a depth of thinking and a deep, consistent framework of assumptions around those conclusions that are very different from what you might be used to. That's why, when you hear those ideas out of context, it can sound unrealistic.

Libertarianism is a political philosophy of peace and nonviolence. When you take the principles of nonviolence to their logical ends, some of the conclusions are startling. If you have a few minutes to open your mind, this book can help you get started in understanding.

The first section will address some of the more outlandish misconceptions and pertinent concerns that most people have. The second section will explore the concept of liberty a bit more deeply, the third will talk about government, while the fourth section will explain about how society might be organized in a libertarian world. The last section will deal with economics.

In a small book like this, we can only scratch the surface of many topics. Many of the chapters have references that can be used to start a deeper investigation. Some of these are online references, for which I have not provided URLs – use your favorite search engine to find the current location of these works. This is not a complete tour of libertarian ideas, nor is any attempt made to furnish a completely footnoted reference work. However, by starting with the suggested books at the end of the sections, the interested reader can make a very deep exploration of these ideas.

Libertarianism offers a different perspective on the world, and an alternative to the exponentially growing interference of government in private life. It is my sincere hope that this little book will intrigue you, and even if you disagree with the ideas presented, you will come away with a deeper understanding of the principles of a free society.

Crazy Misconceptions

The mainstream press is full of crazy misconceptions and misrepresentations of libertarianism. So let's tackle to some of them.

1

Ok, so what is libertarianism?

You already know. Everything you need to know about libertarianism you learned in preschool: don't hurt the other kids. Don't take their stuff. Don't lie. If you hurt someone, make it right.

In other words, don't use force, threats, or coercion on nonviolent people. Libertarians call this the **non-aggression principle**. This is the core of libertarianism; in effect, everything else follows as logical consequences of this central idea.

Sounds reasonable. Most people, most likely you included, live their lives this way. So what's the controversy?

Well, libertarians take this non-aggression stuff seriously. I mean, *really* seriously. Libertarians think that *everyone*, *all the time*, has to conform to this principle, including, and *most especially*, people who work for the government.

This is where the controversy lies. Libertarians believe that just because you got a new job in the government, you did not suddenly acquire the permission to break the most fundamental moral precepts of human society. This idea runs contrary to almost everything that people are led to believe, which is usually that the government's goals are noble, so they should be able to do whatever they want. So it takes a little bit of time, patience, and soul-searching to really understand it. Shopenhauer said, "All truth passes through three stages. First, it is ridiculed. Second, it is violently opposed. Third, it is accepted as being self-evident." Let's see if we can at least get past stage one!

So how would it work? How would a society look where no one - even the government - is allowed to initiate force against anyone else? Libertarian thinkers have spent a lot of time relentlessly exploring the non-aggression principle and refining ideas of what kind of society would conform to this principle. Some of the conclusions, at first glance, are startling and non-intuitive.

But first, let's review some of the most common misunderstanding.

2

So everyone just does what they want?

Yes and no. You can do what you want *as long as you obey the non-aggression principle*. You can't hurt people. You can't take their stuff. You can't lie. You can't use coercion or violence. But within those bounds, you are free to live as you like.

Let's mention right up front that this is not pacifism, which is the belief that no violence should ever be employed for any reason. Most libertarians believe that once a person has stepped outside the law and initiated aggression (they hurt someone, stole or ruined their property, or committed fraud) then force against that person is justified — just not desirable! Throughout this book, when we say "no one can use force," it is understood that the rest of the sentence reads "against nonviolent individuals."

3

So libertarianism means no law? No rules?

No, no, no, and no. Human societies *need* law and rules. Concrete rules are necessary to order society. Lawless civilization is an oxymoron, a contradiction. There will always be people who seek to take advantage of those weaker than themselves. Law is necessary to keep bad actors from aggressing against the weak. Laws should deter and punish violations of the non-aggression principle, what lawyers today call *malum in se*. The law itself would be organized like the common law, which originated in the practices of the courts of the English kings before 1066 AD.
(See Richard Maybury's *Whatever Happened to Justice* for more details.)

Of course, laws alone don't prevent violence - they must be enforceable and enforced. Therefore a functioning society needs an institution strong enough to enforce the law and protect the weak. In recent centuries, that institution has been the government. But does it have to be the government? This is actually a very interesting, and very controversial, topic. For now, let's keep going, and we'll come back to this later.

To continue to explore this idea, read:
Richard Maybury, *Whatever Happened to Justice?*

4

But then it's rugged individualists, each man for himself, not caring about anyone else, right?

Absolutely not! This is a common straw-man argument that the uninformed (or the malicious) use to discredit libertarianism. The idea of the rugged individual, who needs no one, cares for no one, and is a law unto himself is definitely not what libertarianism is. Libertarians revel in the web of complex human relationships - in fact, a good reason for libertarianism is to allow humans to associate and cooperate as much as they wish.

On the contrary, libertarians, and especially economists of the Austrian School, are enthralled by the beauty of societal organization. A key belief of the entire movement is that you can freely interact with and trade with other people, and that doing so, advances all of society. The entire economy, and thus our whole way of life, depends upon the intricate dance of cooperation and competition with other people. Without it, we die: just think how long you could survive without buying *anything* from another person. Libertarians delight in the ingenuity of human beings to solve their problems, and simply think that they should be free to do so. People will still form families, communities, companies, even nations, but they will do so *freely* and *not* under the threat of violence.

Of course, if you *want* to be a rugged individualist, free from all bonds, you could be. As long as you don't hurt anyone, don't take their stuff, and don't lie. No one could force you to associate, or not associate, with anyone. But the vast majority of people would chose to be associated with other people voluntarily. In fact, most libertarian philosophers believe that a free society would have much *tighter* bonds of family and community than we have now – in the absence of state-sponsored safety nets, people would once again take responsibility to care for those around them.

5

Yeah but, libertarians don't care about the disadvantaged. They would just let the poor die in the street!

Don't be ridiculous. Libertarians are not gleefully celebrating the misfortune of others. They might say they are against federal programs for poverty relief, however. This is misrepresented as not "caring" about the poor.

Underlying this objection is a false assumption, a bit of illogical thinking that comes up in many arguments. The thinking goes like this. We have a problem - say, poverty - and we want to solve it. We have two plans. Plan A is a mandatory, nationwide, one-size-fits-all, taxpayer-funded, bureaucratically-administered, multi-billion dollar federal program. Plan B, the only other conceivable option, is to do nothing. Therefore, if you oppose Plan A, you hate the poor and want them to die.

A few seconds of thought, even by someone who is not a professional social worker, should be able to discover dozens of other ways to help people in poverty. In fact, there are likely thousands of ways to help the poor. So opposing nationwide, one-size-fits-all mandatory poverty reduction programs is *not* the same as saying we should do nothing.

In addition, most libertarians truly believe that those centralized programs are incredibly inefficient and expensive, and actually *hurt* the recipients more than they help. And there's a lot of data to back that up.

Beware of this "if you don't support the massive federal program, you support doing nothing" argument. It is *false*, unhelpful, unproductive, and just plain mean and narrow-minded. But you will see this argument made *everywhere.* (For example, if you mention that a multi-decade war is not the best way to defeat terrorism, the likely response is, "So then we do nothing?")

Getting back to poverty, any of us can be down on our luck at some time in our life. Few of us would consent to live in a society where *nothing* is done to help struggling people. Libertarians believe that the best help is local help - starting with family, friends, church, community, charity. If government involvement is necessary, which is debatable, it should start at this local level.

To continue to explore this idea, read:
Mary Ruwart, *Healing Our World*

6

Okay. But you guys actually *like* capitalism!

Sure. Capitalism has saved more people's lives, lifted more people out of poverty, cured more diseases, and improved people's living conditions more than any other institution in the history of mankind. There's a reason that for 200,000 years, living conditions barely improved, but within two centuries of discovering capitalism, per capita wealth increased by more than a factor of 100 - even though the population of the world increased tenfold! China recently lifted hundreds of millions out of extreme poverty in just a generation after they embraced capitalism. The percent of the world's population living in abject poverty (those living on $1/day) fell from 84% in 1820 to less than 10% today, despite that the population of the world increased over seven times. All of that wealth was generated by capitalism.

People have always tried to improve their lives, to "get ahead." People have always hoped their children would not have to suffer as they did. To progress, human beings *must* specialize, and once you've specialized, you *must* obtain what others have produced (since you are not producing it yourself). For millennia, a common way to do that was to find another tribe, beat them up or kill them, and take their stuff. People who traded peacefully with each other often found themselves under the heel of king or warlord – a government – that took most of whatever excess they produced by force, leaving them little to trade. The history of mankind is a series of fights over resources and wealth. With the advent of capitalism came a different way - a more *peaceful* way - to get ahead. Produce something that other people value, and sell it to them, then use the money to buy what you want from other people. You are *cooperating* with others instead of killing them. Without trade and capitalism, we revert back to raiding and pillaging - force and coercion.

What most people don't understand is the difference between capitalism and *crony* capitalism. Crony capitalism is where various parties use the power of the government - which is coercion, force, and aggression - to acquire or protect wealth, often through onerous regulations (large corporations are often the author of, or at least highly influence, regulations that affect their industry). In today's world, no other area of the economy is so highly regulated and tightly integrated (through the Federal Reserve, for example) with the government as financeThe richest counties in the United States are those surrounding Washington DC where many defense contractors live, and near New York City where financial firms are located. This is not a coincidence .

We'll talk more about economics later.

To continue to explore this idea, read:
C. Bradley Thompson, *Socialism vs Capitalism: Which is the Moral System (online article)*
Hunter Lewis, *Economics in Three Lessons*

7

But why are libertarians so critical of government?

Libertarians have two basic problems with the government: the institutionalized use of force and violence (if you stubbornly refuse to obey, you will end up in jail or dead), and the fact that it is the monopoly supplier of the services it provides.

Government grants itself the right to hurt and kill people, to take their stuff, to lock them up in cages, to lie and commit fraud. This violates the very basis of the non-aggression principle. So it is very natural that libertarians are not too happy with government. Simply getting a new job with the Drug Enforcement Administration should not give you the right to bust down your neighbor's door, point a gun at him and lock him up in a cage for smoking a substance that you disapprove of. *Everyone* should be bound by the non-aggression principle.

Governments do provide many essential services: administration of justice and national defence being among the most important. Depending on where you live, the government may also supply roads, medicine, educational facilities, water, fire departments, emergency response teams, parks, etc. No one has a problem with these services -

they are all wonderful things! The problem with government supplying them is that government is a monopoly supplier. Protected from any competition (and often able to compel people with force to use - and pay for - their services), it is inevitable that quality suffers and and the focus turns inward to bureaucratic matters rather than outwards towards customer service. The fabled poor service at the Department of Motor Vehicles is the usual emblematic example.

Another objection to government coercion is that it truly appears to almost always *backfire* - in using violence to protect, we end up hurting those we meant to help. For a description of these effects, with tons of data to back them up, see Ruwart's book, below.

Society *needs* rules, laws, and the protection of the weak. Libertarian thinkers have spent a lot of time trying to figure out how to arrange *peaceful* societies, with a non-coercive government. These philosophers have also pondered whether we can have competition in the provision of government-supplied services like road and highway service - if the DMV employee abuses you, take your business (and your money) elsewhere! It's not an easy problem to solve. Not everyone believes it is solvable. But more on that later.

To continue to explore this idea, read:
Mary Ruwart, *Healing Our World*

Richard   Maybury,   *Whatever   Happened   to   Justice*
Frederik Bastiat, *The Law*

8

Yeah, but every country where government collapses falls into chaos! It really is *Mad Max!*

Agreed - you cannot take a society that completely relies on government for law and order, eliminate that government, and expect a spontaneous flowering of a peaceful and private law-abiding society. Libertarianism is not magic, and it's best to abandon magical thinking and get practical. If you wanted to change society from gasoline-powered cars to electric cars, you don't start by shutting down all the gas stations overnight — same with government services.

As we'll talk about later, some libertarians think that the institution of government has an unstoppable tendency to expand and gravitate toward tyranny, and if we want to keep our liberty we have to find ways to deliver the services of government through peaceful, voluntary means. If our goal was to replace the state with non-coercive institutions, those institutions would have to be designed, built up, and strengthened over time, before they could take over.

9

Then what exactly is the libertarian political agenda?

Ah, this is a really important point. It's important to separate the *philosophy* of libertarianism with libertarian *politics*. The two are very frequently confused, even by – perhaps especially by — libertarians themselves, resulting in a lot of avoidable acrimony.

The philosophy of libertarianism is the long-running discussion of how we might obtain the ideal society, free of institutionalized coercion and force. Since a lot of this is a thought experiment, not everyone agrees on how this ideal might be realized. Some believe that we can *never* eliminate all coercion from society, but even these individuals agree that a violence-free society is a kind of "north star," the ideal that we should strive for and by which we should measure all our actions. Some of libertarian philosophy is deductive - starting with the non-aggression principle and logically thinking through how that would work. Other parts are observational - for example, we know a lot about economics and how a free-market economy performs.

The politics of libertarianism deals with more immediate and practical concerns: which public policies should be implemented today? Even if libertarian *philosophy* demands a tiny or even non-existent state, *politically* we cannot just disband the government tomorrow. We must deal with the world as it is. Political libertarianism is how we make the slow march toward the ideals that philosophical libertarianism has shown us.

These two realms are constantly confused, even among libertarians (of both the political and philosophical bent), as well as among critics. People read that Murray Rothbard advocated a society without a state and they shout "Don't vote for the libertarians! They're going to disband the government! Those libertarians are crazy!" Don't fall for the hype. Libertarianism has had some brilliant thinkers — they might be wrong, but they were not crazy.

Liberty

The core idea of libertarianism is, of course, liberty. So let's explore the idea of liberty and how it becomes libertarianism.

10

What does liberty mean?

Ah, liberty! As Americans, we cherish it! We wish "liberty and justice for all" at the end of the Pledge of Allegiance. Patrick Henry, a Founding Father, wanted to die if he couldn't have it. We even have a whole statue for it!

The Oxford English Dictionary defines liberty as "the state of being free within society from oppressive restrictions imposed by authority on one's way of life, behavior, or political views." Of course, there are some slippery bits here: who is authority? And what kind of restrictions might be "oppressive"?   There is room for reasonable disagreement here - one person's "oppressive" could be another person's "reasonable." We'll try to find a cleaner definition in the upcoming chapters.

Liberty is also an idea. For most of history, the vast majority of humanity accepted that they were either owned by someone, or owed their existence to their masters - kings, religious authorities, local warlords, anyone who wished to dominate them and use their labor and property as their own. One lens through which you can view history is the struggle of power vs. liberty. Power usually won.

During the 16th and 17th century, a new philosophy began to develop, which stated that people were *supposed* to be free, that it was natural and right to live in a state of liberty. That didn't go over too well — the well-connected and aristocratic types felt that the "commoners" their "guidance" in order to better themselves. But over time, the philosophy gained adherents, including the Founders of the United States of America.

11

What is the basic belief of libertarianism?

Libertarianism can be founded entirely upon the *non-aggression principle*. The non-aggression principle states that no human being has the right to initiate aggression against the person or property of another human being. In other words, don't hurt people. Don't take their stuff. Don't lie to them.

While most people think that these statements are fine and valuable, libertarians *really* take this seriously. *No one* can initiate force — that includes the government. Brilliant philosophers, over many centuries, have pondered how we could build a society free of coercive violence. This is what we are exploring in this book.

Libertarians are not pacifists, however. They firmly believe in the use of violence, when and if necessary, against someone who has already initiated the violence. If you steal a libertarian's wallet, you can expect a punch in the nose.

Yet another way of saying this is the old saw: "you can do whatever you want as long as you don't interfere with other people's right to do the same", or that all actions should be voluntary. Christians and Jews might like to think of libertarianism as the secular part of the Ten Commandments: "Thou shalt not kill. Thou shalt not bear false witness. Thou shalt not steal." The ideas of libertarianism have been around for a really, really long time.

To continue to explore this idea, read:
Richard Maybury, *Whatever Happened to Justice*
Mary Ruwart, *Healing Our World*
Laura Nicolae, *TedEx HarvardCollege Entry: The Non-Aggression Principle (YouTube upload)*

12

Who grants us liberty? Where do these rights come from?

Philosophers debate these questions, and have proposed several answers. Some argue simply that liberty is proven to be the best way that we know of to give everyone as much wealth and opportunity as possible - this is a **utilitarian** argument. However, here we'll take on a moral argument - the idea of **natural rights**. Natural rights are basically what you read about in the Declaration of Independence: "We hold these truths to be self-evident, that all men are created equal, and are endowed by their Creator with certain unalienable Rights, that among these are Life, Liberty, and the Pursuit of Happiness." Note that rights are unalienable - in other words, they come from our Creator, or from Nature if you prefer, and *cannot* be taken away.

Natural rights theory says that, simply by virtue of being a human being, you are the owner of several things: your body, your mind, your time, and the fruits of your labors. Let's take these one at a time. First, let's define what we mean by "own". In all cases, when we say you own something we mean you are allowed to do with it as you will, without the permission of others. You are the final arbiter of how that object is used, and you are responsible for it.

You own your own body. It has been pointed out that the alternative to owning your body is that someone else, either one person or many, own your body. This is called slavery. Hopefully we can all agree that the opposite of slavery is a good place to start!

You own your own mind. Your thoughts and opinions are your own, and no one else has a right to tell you what to think, how to live, etc. The Thought Police are always a scary, um, thought.

You own your time. In essence, time is life. We all have a finite amount of time on this planet. You should be able to decide what to do with your time here, and with whom you spend it. Someone who steals your time from you is literally stealing your life.

You own the fruits of your labor. Labor takes time, and time is life. If you go into the forest and pick up some wild apples, they are now yours. If you buy some lumber and make a nice piece of furniture, it's now yours. If anyone takes it from you without permission, it is theft. Again, if someone *else* owns the fruits of your labor, then you are a slave.

To continue to explore this idea, read:
Murray Rothbard, *For a New Liberty*

Aaron Ross Powell and Grant Babcock, ed.,
Arguments for Liberty

13

What are the big political issues for libertarians?

Given that libertarians believe in the non-aggression principle and in everyone's right to life, liberty, and property, it follows that the biggest issues would be the most egregious violations of those basic rights.

War (Foreign)

Governments fighting wars of aggression is probably the top issue. After all, people are *dying*, by the tens and hundreds of thousands. Since the advent of modern warfare, most of the dead have been civilians. From a libertarian perspective this is mass murder, and it is just not okay to murder people unless the threat to you is real and imminent. Nowadays, governments murder people routinely to protect their "interests" overseas. Untold amounts of money is wasted, whole countries ruined, and generations of people have their lives destroyed.

War (Domestic)

Aggressively policing nonviolent crimes, and especially the War on Drugs, is another blatant assault against liberty. Locking people in cages because they are smoking a plant you disapprove of (and shooting them if they resist) has no place in a society based on liberty. Once again, the lives of hundreds of thousands of people (mostly minorities) have been ruined, and untold amounts of money wasted (in the US, about 80% of law-enforcement budgets go for drug laws - not murderers, rapists, and thieves). An epidemic of violence has been exported to multiple countries. Far more people are killed in the War on Drugs than die from drug overdoses. If people are not infringing on the life, liberty, or property of others when they take a recreational drug, there is no crime.

Economic Interventionism

The Federal Reserve was formed in 1913. The value of the US dollar has fallen by about 97% since then. This means the government has confiscated 97% of the money of the population via inflation. Don't you think that's enough? Since abandoning the gold standard in the early 1970s, real wages, corrected for inflation, have stagnated while productivity continued to climb. This is not a coincidence. Who do you think got all that extra wealth? The government's "management" of the economy almost always leaves everyone worse off - except, of course, bankers and politicians. People have to earn a living to survive, and to have their earnings stolen like this is unconscionable.

Criminal Justice System

Our criminal justice system is running amok here in the US. Prosecuting attorneys have almost unlimited leeway. Prosecuting teams can break laws with near impunity, and frequently they aggressively attack defendants with numerous, punitive charges and then plea bargain down to get a "confession." Minorities are arrested and imprisoned at much higher rates than whites. Millions of nonviolent offenders fill our prisons. Innocent men are on death row. Meanwhile, laws like sovereign immunity protects government workers who break the law. They go free while whistleblowers are imprisoned.

When the scales are tilted away from defendants, there cannot really be said to be justice. When the law is not applied equally to prosecution and defense, there cannot really be said to be justice. This is one of the main reasons that improverished and minority people are losing faith in the American experiment, and deciding that civil society doesn't deserve their allegiance.

The law must apply to everyone equally, including prosecution teams and politicians. If a prosecutor breaks the law or infringes on the liberty of a suspect, they have committed a crime. Nonviolent citizens should not be locked up in cages. Without a basis of sound law, a healthy society cannot exist.

It would be even better if we could switch from **punitive** justice to **restorative** justice, but that's a discussion for later.

Surveillance

The huge surveillance state being built up in modern times is a tremendous threat to liberty. It has been estimated that the Federal Criminal Code is so big and complex that most people commit on average three felonies a day. Now that the government can record everything you do, say, view, and read, it's quite easy to find a law that you've broken. With this access to data, if you become an irritant to government, they can check your records and fabricate a charge at any time.

To continue to explore this idea, read:
Harry Silverglate and Alan M. Dershowitz, *Three Felonies a Day*,
Cato Institute, *Criminal Justice* (online reading list compiled by Tim Lynch)
Scott Horton, *Fool's Errand*
Murray Rothbard, *What Has Government Done to Our Money?*
Richard Maybury, *Whatever Happened to Penny Candy?*
Frederic Bastiat, *The Law*

14

What is the difference between "liberalism" and "libertarianism"?

The tradition of liberty was called "liberalism" in Europe (still is, actually). But in the United States, "liberal" came to describe left-wing political positions. The idea of liberty is not a left-wing idea. So a new name was needed in America, and the word "libertarianism" was coined. But it is mostly synonymous with what Europeans call "classical liberalism."

(Here is a good place to point out that not everyone who claims they are a libertarian actually understands the philosophy of libertarianism. For example, libertarian philosophy supports the decriminalization of recreational drugs like marijuana. There have been countless people whose politics go like this: "I like to smoke pot. Libertarians want to legalize pot!?! Ok, I'm a libertarian!" Then they tell everyone they are a libertarian without having even the slightest inkling what they are talking about. Similarly on the issues of taxes and war. Be aware that these people may not have a deep understanding of libertarian thought.)

So liberty is not a left-wing idea. In fact, hopefully you now recognize that it's not a right-wing idea either. Although left-wing ideology shares some important ideas with libertarianism (like civil rights, anti-war, freedom in your private life), so does right-wing ideology (like private property, smaller government, and freedom in your economic dealings). Libertarianism is not "centrist" (half way between the left and the right) either - it lies perpendicular to the line between left and right, off to the side. It is often said that libertarians are better liberals than liberals, and better conservatives than conservatives — and hence loathed by both sides!

From the perspective of libertarianism, the left and the right both have some pieces right, and some pieces wrong. Mainly what they have wrong is the employment of government force to shove their agendas down the throats of their political opponents.

15

Wouldn't a libertarian society be libertine?

So libertarians are European liberals but not American liberals. But aren't they all just libertines? Wouldn't a libertarian society be Sodom and Gomorrah all over again?

There seems to be an unstated thought behind this fear: "Sure, I'm a good person, and so are my friends. But everyone else is pretty nasty. Society would go to you-know-where pretty fast if the government wasn't here to knock sense into people." Bastiat talks about how politicians divide the world into two groups - the commoners (vile, slothful, left alone they will descend into barbarism) and themselves, the politicians and statesmen (the brilliant guiding lights, uplifting mankind for its own betterment, guardians of civilization).

Ugh, please. The vast majority of people want to have a nice life, raise a family, and contribute something back to the world. The pattern of thought that "I'm nice but everyone else is not" leads us to a lot of unproductive solutions. Without government, people have, and would continue to, write symphonies, help the poor, make scientific discoveries, love their children, and in general live life as humans have for millenia.

In a libertarian society, one would have to live with the consequences of one's own behavior. If a person decided to spend their days doing drugs, going to wild parties, etc., that would be fine - but if you don't spend some time earning a living, they are going to be caught out without food on the table.

A truly libertarian society would likely be a more socially conservative society, because the safety net would be quite different. There would still be a safety net, as families and communities supported each other. In the US, before WWII, there were even "mutual aid societies" where several hundred or thousand people came together voluntarily to self-insure their members. When someone hit on hard times, other members of the society would try to help by finding them work, taking them in, or the society might even pay out cash payments. But in such a small group where "everyone knows everyone else", really crazy behavior would not be tolerated, because other members of the group are liable. So family and community ties are likely to be much stronger in a libertarian society.

And if you wanted to go it alone and party like there's no tomorrow, there might not be any tomorrow for you. That is your right. If it turns out badly, you might be in the position on subsisting on the welfare of strangers.

To continue to explore this idea, read:
Frederic Bastiat, *The Law*
David Beito, *From Mutual Aid to Welfare State*

Government and Law

If the tapestry of history is the struggle between liberty and power, power is represented by the state. Generally, the state claims a monopoly on the use of violence in a geographical area (in fact, this is often the definition of the state used by libertarians). In fact, every law and regulation represents a form of aggression, if not complied with: try not paying your taxes and see how long you can stay at liberty. Either they will take it from you forcibly, or they will send men with guns to lock you up in a cage, and if you resist, they will kill you. So every government rule is backed by the threat of force. George Washington was reputed to have said "Government is not reason, it is not eloquence — it is force. Like fire, it is a dangerous servant and a fearful master; never for a moment should it be left to irresponsible action."

16

Libertarians are all anarchists, right? They don't think government is necessary?

Although some libertarians describe themselves as anarchists, the word is again used inappropriately as a strawman argument to discredit libertarianism.

What comes to your mind when you think of "anarchy"? Probably bands of masked left-wing maniacs, throwing Molotov cocktails, smashing windows and lighting people's cars on fire. Here is where you can one-up the pathetic mainstream commentary and use your own brain: how is this behavior compatible with the non-aggression principle (don't hurt people, don't take their stuff, don't lie)? Quite obviously, it is not. Therefore libertarians will *not* support this sort of activity.

Once again, multiple concepts are likely conflated in your mind, those of **government** and **governance**. Governance, the institutions that protect law and order, enforce contracts, and make sure that criminals are caught, is absolutely necessary to a peaceful and prosperous society. A government, an organization that claims the sole legitimate use of violence and the ultimate decision-making authority is, perhaps, not necessary.

What some libertarians believe is that we can *govern* ourselves without a *government.* That we could use private agreements, contracts, insurance, and other-yet-to-be-invented ideas to make sure society remains ordered, and the strong do not take advantage of the weak.

A libertarian society would be a hard core law-and-order society - except only *serious* crimes would be punishable: murder, rape, assault, theft, fraud, etc. However having a vegetable garden in your front yard or seeing the "wrong" kind of doctor, or refusing to finance or fight in a war you don't believe in would not be crimes in law.

As mentioned above, some libertarians admit no legitimate role for the state; in other words, they are anarchists. Others feel that a small, constrained government (like that described in the US Constitution) is desirable. Because they agitate for minimal government, the term "minarchist" came to be used, somewhat humorously.

The state currently delivers some essential services - building roads, supplying water, defending national borders, etc. Anarchists don't want to go without those services — it's crazy to think we could all protect our own liberty without some sort of structured organization to help. But they want those services to be provided by the private sector, so that citizens have a choice. Don't like the job your police are doing? Fire them and hire a new firm (sort of like private security guards today). Any monopoly supplier becomes self-absorbed and disdainful of its customers over time, and the government is not immune to this. Currently, if you don't like the job the government does, you can vote against them, but that has little effect if a majority of others don't agree. But in a competitive landscape, you can just switch providers. For example, if you don't like the job that Ford does, buy a Chevy. You don't need to wait for 51% of the population to agree with you. Competition and free markets allow citizens to vote with their wallets.

Minarchists might agree, but they realize there may be enormous practical difficulties in provisioning these services entirely from the private sector, for example the administration of justice or environmental law. For this reason, they conclude that a minimal government must remain to protect our liberty and provide military defense.

Anarchists like Murray Rothbard disagree. Rothbard quipped that he had spent his whole life trying, and failing, to come up with a self-consistent, logical explanation of why certain services should be provided by the state and others should not. Providing *any* service opens the door to *all* services, with no logical stopping point. Also, he was unable to come up with a way of creating a limited government that would not have incentive to grow without bound, aggregating all power to itself.

It's fascinating to think how private provisioning of *everything* might work in a totally free society. However, this is so far from our current situation of all-powerful states that it remains simply an interesting thought experiment. We can't really know what sort of ingenious solutions some entrepreneur might come up with over the course of decades. But dismissing libertarianism because you can't agree with or foresee the final end is throwing out the baby with the bathwater.

One thing is for sure - one simply cannot "end government tomorrow" and think that society will somehow spontaneously blossom into a peaceful and just form. Before government is rolled back, a lot of work must be done into setting up and testing the institutions that will replace it, especially those concerned with law and order, justice, and crime. Countries that have had their central governments destroyed overnight have almost all devolved into chaos, as the criminal elements sense their chance to seize power.

We'll discuss this more in the Society section of this book.

To continue to explore this idea, read:
Murray Rothbard, *For a New Liberty*
Hans Hoppe, *State or Private Law Society* (online article)
Robert Murphy, *Chaos Theory*

17

Then what is the proper role of government?

In minarchist thinking, the government should primarily be protecting our liberties; in other words, the primary function of the government should be to see that the non-aggression principle is obeyed. This means it is only concerned with the administration of justice — police, courts, judges, etc. People call this the "night watchman" state. Or you could say it is simply following the actual intent of the US Constitution.

Another area for state involvement is foreign relations.   This includes national defense, and potentially diplomacy: as long as other regions in the world have states, we probably also need one. If every society was libertarian, there wouldn't be any large aggressors to defend against and likely these functions of the state would fall away, since only a state can marshall the resources to invade a large territory.

In any event, most libertarians agree that the smaller the state, the better.

18

What is so great about small government?

Actually there are multiple areas of "small" to consider. Small in terms of authority, small in terms of geographical region, and small in terms of finances and resources.

When a government gets large in terms of authority, and begins interfering in many realms of private and economic life, it becomes wasteful in terms of money and menacing in terms of liberty. Politicians start to feel they are like kings, or benevolent overseers, who must instruct the base masses in the proper ways to live. Also, the more the government regulates, the more money corporations can make by sending lobbyists and buying policy, and the more the government becomes beholden to these special interests at the cost of the average person. If government didn't have the authority to intervene in so many areas of society, corporations wouldn't bother to bribe it, and instead would go back to focusing on providing better products and services for customers.

In terms of geography, a smaller area will have a less powerful government, simply because it has less citizens to tax and therefore less money. Also, a smaller jurisdiction means that if the government starts to abuse its citizens, they can more easily leave — vote with their feet. And of course, there's likely to be less corruption if the mayor lives down the street and is seen by everyone at local community events.

In terms of financial resources, the less the government has, the fewer wars there will be, and the fewer people will die. Also, less of the citizen's wealth will be squandered on building bombs, blowing up buildings, rebuilding them, and then blowing them up again. A fiscally constrained government, like that of Switzerland, would focus on protecting the people's rights, property, and liberty, instead of adventuring into areas it has no business in.

In a nutshell, small government means less violation of the non-aggression principle and more liberty.

19

But then who's going to protect us from the big, bad corporations?

Every large corporation spends excessive sums of money, in the tens of millions of dollars, on lobbying the government. Why do you think they do that? Do you think they are just very civic minded, or do they expect a financial return on that investment? And with corporate donors financing the campaigns of aspiring politicians, do you really think that once elected those politician will put the welfare of the average person ahead of those donors?

When a small company starts to grow quite large, it becomes more and more difficult to stay on top of its game. As the employee count becomes larger, the company becomes more and more bureaucratic, ossified, and slow. It starts to look inward to bureaucratic and political empire-building, and less and less to the customers. Generally, large companies would mostly collapse, going the way of IBM, Eastman-Kodak, K-Mart, Borders, Blockbusters… A few, like Apple, might thrive, if they can remember to continuously delight their customers. But this requires continued innovation and experimentation. That's *hard*, especially in a large company.

This is why most companies, when they get large, turn to lobbying the government. Since the government grants itself the right to pass almost arbitrary legislation and regulation, the opportunities to lock in profits are almost too good to resist. Studies have shown that the majority of legislation passed by the government is actually proposed by the companies in that market, and that most regulation has the effect of protecting the incumbent large corporations from competition and from their customers' demands.

In a libertarian society, of course, the ability of politicians to protect their big corporate donors would be limited or non-existent. Companies would have to delight their customers, or be taken down a peg. Without crony capitalist regulation, corporations are entirely at the mercy of their customers.

It's also quite likely that the system of limited liability would be done away with in a libertarian society. Currently, the government grants a kind of immunity to officers of a corporation. If "the corporation" pollutes your land, then "the corporation" is punished, as if it was a person. But of course, there were individual officers of that company that made the decision to dump that poison on your land. In a libertarian society, it is likely that they would be *personally* responsible to the plaintiffs for decisions taken in bad faith. That alone would put a huge damper on bad behavior.

It's one thing if the company is fined $100 million, it's quite another thing for an executive to lose his life savings and have to move into a low-rent condo.

Corporations that infringe on people's rights, by polluting or by producing defective or fraudulent products, would be prosecuted of course. But there is always the problem of a corporation being so big and powerful that it would be able to corrupt the justice system. Of course, this is the exact problem we have now, so this is not unique to a libertarian system.

20

What is the state?

We touched on this before, but one definition of the state is the organization that claims a monopoly on physical violence and force in a defined geographical area. This definition might strike you as way out there, as it did me the first time I heard it, but turn it over in your mind for the next couple days. As you think about it, you may start to realize it has some truth to it.

A variation on this definition is that the state is the organization that in a defined geographical area claims the final decision-making authority, including on matters concerning itself. For example, the state is the only organization that decides its own income (which others are obligated to provide, under threat of violence).

Another definition involves the terms "political means" and "economic means." In order to survive, people need and want stuff - land, food, water, clothing, cell phones, cars, etc. In the final analysis, there are only two ways to get stuff. One is to peacefully and voluntarily trade what you *can* make with other people in order to get what you *want*. This is called the "economic means". The other way is to take it, forcibly, from others who already have it. This is called the "political means".

With these terms now defined, we can say that the state is the formal organization of the political means. The government uses taxes, inflation, and outright confiscation to "earn" a living. For non-state actors, if you want more than you have, you have to produce more: work longer hours, work smarter, get a promotion, etc. A company needs to serve more customers: expand the market, make better products, make more products more efficiently. The state can just decide it needs more, and take it. The state is the only organization that unilaterally determines its own revenue.

To continue to explore this idea, read:
Murray Rothbard, *Anatomy of the State*
Franz Oppenheimer, *The State*

21

What's the difference between the state and the country?

One thing to be careful of is the confusion, deliberately fostered, between the state and the country. The country is a geographical region, with hundreds of millions of residents in the case of the US, who share close connections in terms of language, culture, and economy. The state, on the other hand, is a set of organizations belonging to and associated with the government, including closely affiliated industries like finance and the military-industrial complex.

You can understand the difference here by thinking about the fabled "government shutdowns". This is trumpeted as "when the country stopped working". However, almost everyone went to work during the shutdowns, got paid, had dinner - in short, the life of the *country* goes on. The state is not the country.

One place where this is often confused is in foreign policy. The media talks about "America's interests overseas." Do you have much interest there? The "interests" in question are interests of the government, or more broadly, the state, not the people. These interests generally boil down to opportunities for the state to increase its power.

This gets even creepier when war breaks out. The propaganda makes it sound like the state is charging to the defense of the American people — "Defend America!". But if you examine events more soberly, you realize that it's the *people* rushing to the defense of the *state*! The "interests" we are protecting are those of the state, and usually only a small group within the state, at that. It was not always so — war used to be private. Murray Rothbard has written about the moment when the average citizen first became co-opted to protect the state.

At one point in the 2016 election, Hillary Clinton pointed out that she was more qualified to be commander-in-chief of the United States than Donald Trump. The Cato Institute, a libertarian think tank, pointed out that the United States does not have a commander-in-chief. The armed forces do, but you and I, who are not serving in the military, do *not* have a commander-in-chief. Jousting over words perhaps, but it shows how these concepts can be confused and few people even notice.

To continue to explore this idea, read:
Murray Rothbard, *For a New Liberty*

22

Why don't libertarians like the state?

Remember the non-aggression principle: don't hurt people, don't take their stuff, don't lie. We naturally feel that this should apply to everyone equally. The biggest problem with the state is that they exempt themselves from this moral precept. Individuals working for the state quite frequently hurt, kill, and imprison people, take their possessions, and commit fraud.

They even have official-sounding names for this, like "sovereign immunity" and "civil asset forfeiture". The question is why do we as citizens permit a small group of people to exempt themselves from the most basic moral guidelines? "We were just implementing official policy" is about as strong a moral defense as the "we were just following orders" used by the Nazis at the Nuremburg Trials.

For example, if you don't like the plant that your neighbor is smoking, you can't morally (or legally) threaten him with a gun and lock him up in a cage, just because you disapprove. However, if you work for the DEA you can.

Libertarians want to live in a society where action is *voluntary*, not coerced. But coercion is the state's middle name. If you don't believe it, try not paying your taxes. Or getting an alternative treatment for cancer. Or giving your children a (too) large amount of your money.

The state is also responsible for most of the violence against humanity. In the 20th century, governments killed hundreds of millions of innocent people. Many people think that the private sector is a horrible aggressor against human life — but if you add up *all* the deaths caused by *every* private company in the last century, it would barely hold a candle to even the smallest war perpetrated by governments. And I don't think General Electric has many people locked up in cages for nonviolent offenses. The number of people imprisoned falsely in the US alone is probably more people than the private sector, in its entirety, harms in a year. Most companies tend to realize that it's bad for business to kill your own customers. Governments have yet to come to that conclusion. And in the US, through civil asset forfeiture, the government steals more from innocent civilians than actual thieves do!

Next time the news talks about crimes, ask yourself which of those are true crimes: murder, assault, rape, robbery, fraud, etc. It's actually quite few. All the other crimes are crimes only in that the state says they are. The state creates criminals. Then they send men with guns to capture them. "See, what would you do without us to capture all these bad guys!"

Even kind-hearted policies generally end up hurting those they were meant to help. Think of a young black man in the US. African-Americans are in general housed by the state in projects; the people in need of this housing are impoverished and most subject to crime. Then the children are sent to often-failing public schools, where they spend most of their time trying not to get beat up. Having survived 12 years of traumatization in that system, and armed with a 4th-grade education, our young man tries to get a job. Without skills, he can't command very much in the labor market, so he needs to start at the bottom and work his way up. But due to minimum wage laws, the bottom rungs of the ladder of opportunity are labelled "Keep Off" — if he agrees to work for too little, men with guns will come and lock up his employer in a cage. So no job. He can't start his own business, because licensing laws make the costs too high. However, his neighborhood's drug dealers seem to have nice cars and lots of girlfriends — thanks to the War on Drugs making profits higher than natural. But when he gets involved in dealing drugs, DEA agents come with guns and lock him up in a cage, where he is traumatized further. When he finally gets out of jail, he realizes that firms are forbidden by law from hiring ex-felons to "protect the community". What chance does this guy have? All of this violence comes from the actions of government.

Once the state is unleashed from its constitutional shackles, it tends to grow without bound. Few governments stop and say, "Whoops, we got too big, time to downsize". The US Federal Register (the list of federal rules and regulations) has grown from 107,000 pages in the 1950s to over 820,000 pages in 2010 and is still growing exponentially. Budgets and debt have increased faster than GDP. This can't go on forever - and what can't go on forever will eventually stop.

To continue to explore this idea, read:
Walter Williams, *The State Against Blacks*
Richard Maybury, *World War I* and *World War II*
Lew Rockwell, *Against the State*

23

But doesn't the government take care of us?

"Okay," you say, "so the government has dropped hundreds of thousands of bombs on the Middle East, destroyed multiple nations, ignited conflicts that have killed millions of innocent civilians and turned millions of others into refugees. They have brutally cracked down on recreational drugs, putting millions of nonviolent offenders in jail, and again wrecking several nations. And the Fed just finished orchestrating the transfer of vast amounts of wealth from the lower and middle classes to investment bankers and the politically connected. But look at the nice job they did on the highway system."

Seriously?

To know how much the state cares about you, look at how they prosecute crimes. The government frequently lies to the people with no consequence - who went to jail for the lies leading to the Iraq war? But if you lie to the government, you are in big trouble. Government employees have lied under oath to Congress, have lied to the press, have lied to the UN, have lied to the people. Government prosecutors are often accused of breaking the law and using underhanded techniques, with no consequences. When whistleblowers exposed illegal wrongdoing in Iraq, the existence of illegal torture chambers, or the existence of illegal mass surveillance programs, who went to jail? In each case, the whistleblower was prosecuted mercilessly, and ended up in jail or in exile. No government employee even got a pay cut.

Think about how vigorously the police pursue perpetrators of real crimes like assault, versus people who didn't get a permit or license for their business.

They certainly take care of their own. Just try to stay out of their way.

24

Is government legitimate?

This is actually a fascinating question. Thinkers have often addressed the question of why a small group of people should rule over us. What gives a small group of individuals the right to take the money, liberty, and property of the rest? Why can they use violence and no one else can? What puts them above all moral precepts?

And it turns out, it's really hard to come up with a consistent theory for the legitimacy of government. There is, of course, the divine right of kings - in other words, these people rule because God said so. End of story, nothing else to see here folks. Questioning the rulers' legitimacy is literally blasphemy, and you could very quickly lose your money, your freedom, and even your life, by such questioning.

Fast forward to today, and no one (hopefully) really believes in the Divine Right of Kings anymore. Instead, we have lots of ad hoc theories like the social contract, etc. None of these really hold water under rational scrutiny however. So in fact, there is no theory based on first principles of why government is legitimate.

Of course there are always those who seek power. There are always those who want other people's stuff. There are always those who disapprove of other people's lifestyles, or bank accounts, and long for someone to "bust some heads". And there are plenty of people willing to just watch TV while the former group takes over.   Voila! Instant government.

To continue to explore this idea, read:
Murray Rothbard, *Anatomy of the State*
Cato Institute, *Must You Obey Government?* (online podcast hosted by Aaron Ross Powell and Trevor Burrus)

25

How do libertarians feel about the US Constitution?

Libertarians are divided on the issue of the US Constitution. Some feel it is the greatest device ever created to ensure the liberty of individuals and keep the government limited and under control. Those who fall in this camp think we need to get back to the original intent of the Constitution and put the government genie back in the bottle.

Others feel that the Constitution was a great experiment, but in the end, it was an absolute failure. It was created to keep government in check, but now the US has the largest government in the history of the world, with a $4.5 trillion budget. The US system was meant to have most of the power reside in the states, or local communities, but the Federal government has usurped nearly all that power, and routinely threatens the states — not to mention other countries — if they don't do exactly as instructed.

However, nearly all libertarians believe that life in the US would be better if we could move in the direction of respecting the Constitution.

26

Internationally, are libertarians isolationists?

Libertarians generally advocate a foreign (and domestic) policy of **non-interventionism**. This is often caricatured in the media as **isolationism**. The two are quite different.

Suppose you have some friends, a married couple, who are going through a tough stretch in their marriage. There's a lot of name-calling, accusations, and tears. How do you respond?

One way is to completely ignore them. Don't socialize with them, don't invite them over, don't return their calls, don't answer their invitations. This is an **isolationist** approach.

Another possible response is to march in and tell them how it is. "Now see here," you thunder, "you need to better to your spouse. You can't say things like that. Now kiss and make up." After all, their problem is so obvious to you, as is the solution. You just need to knock some heads and everything will be ok. This is an **interventionist** response.

If you've tried this kind of intervention - advising feuding couples, selecting your children's friends, telling your best friend just what to say to her boss - you know that it often (probably more often than not) backfires, making things worse, and possibly losing you some friends.

The **non-interventionist** approach would be to remain friends, talk to both partners, hear out their grievances, and help where you can without taking sides. Don't ignore them, but don't try to fix them either. Lend emotional support where you can, but let them figure it out themselves. Give opinions (carefully) when asked, but don't offer advice. Generally this is the best approach.

A non-interventionist approach to foreign policy means staying out of other people's conflicts, not taking sides, trading with everyone, talking with everyone, and being friendly with everyone.

A non-interventionist approach to foreign policy generally leaves more people richer and freer, with fewer people dead. Libertarians consider this a good thing.

Society

We are so used to living with governments, and these days, with very powerful governments, that we have a hard time imagining how things could work differently. Many people simply expect the government to solve every single problem, even imaginary ones. So talking about a society without a government, or even a very small one, is very unfamiliar to most people. What would such a society be like?

Imagine if all food was provided by the government. The state owned all the farms, grocery stores, and restaurants, and farmers were civil servants. If, in this world, you suggested privatizing the food system, what would the reaction be? "That's crazy! Food is too important to be left to the private sector! How could we guarantee that our needs would be met? Evil shopowners would demand exorbitant prices - they would make you pay $50 for a loaf of bread, and if you didn't, they'd let you starve to death!" These are "boogeyman stories" — the breathless predictions of the doom that will occur unless the government rescues us from those immoral private sector actors. In actual fact, in our privatized food system, we have so much cheap food that people are dying from obesity.

A truly libertarian society would likely exhibit diversity on a scale unimaginable now. There would be numerous combinations of (voluntary) arrangements between people, increased diversity in the design of neighborhoods and community, and a wide array of lifestyles.

Communities would likely be more tightly knit, because the absence of transfer-payment programs like Social Security means that people would take care of their relatives and neighbors.

27

Do we need rules at all?

Once again let's be clear - if humans are living together, they need rules. A society would have to have some sort of clear, written governing principles. Most of the rules would be refinements of "don't hurt people, don't take their stuff, don't lie" codified to provide concrete guidance. This is how the English common law was created, and the common law formed the basis of the legal system of the newly-forged United States.

So yes, we need rules. Yes, we need a way to enforce them so that the strong don't take advantage of the weak. This is where it gets tricky - how do you have an institution that's powerful enough to stand up to the criminal elements in society, but still prevent that institution itself from abusing its power and becoming an aggressor? Who guards the guardians? Libertarians would point out that the best solution is probably *not* to give an organization a monopoly on the use of force, and then to place that organization mostly above the law. The idea of voluntarily submitting to an enforcement organization, with an option to switch providers at any time - like switching from Ford to Chevy - is probably the most robust solution, albeit very different from what we have today and therefore harder to articulate in its details.

Beware of this area of thought: it's getting so far from our recent experience in statist societies that it's very difficult to predict what sort of issues might arise and how they might be solved. Hence, people just love to argue about this and get into huge fights about different flavors of anarchism and whether crime insurance would solve the problems. Treat all this as interesting discussion and not as proposals to be implemented tomorrow.

To continue to explore this idea, read:
Richard Maybury, *Whatever Happened to Justice*
Murray Rothbard, *For a New Liberty*
Trey Goff, *Voluntaryist Constitution* (online article)
Murray Rothbard, *Are Libertarians Anarchists?* (online article)

28

Are there any examples of libertarian societies?

Unfortunately, there are very few examples. Liberty as a concept only gained popularity quite recently in human history, and so far, the forces of power have generally been victorious over the defenders of liberty. However, there are several that can be cited.

The United States from its founding to about 1913. During this time the Federal government was very weak, and most law was administered by states and localities. People came from all over the world to participate in the awesome prosperity that was unleashed. The United States generated more wealth than had existed in the entire history of the world. In the early 20th century, particularly with the advent of the national income tax and the creation of the Federal Reserve Bank, the groundwork was laid for the eventual destruction of liberty. The US now has the largest government (by spending) that has ever existed in the history of the human race - and they still claim they need more.

Ancient Celtic Ireland (Brehon Law, 2300BC to the 17th century). T Irish had a society that was remarkably free of central power. They developed a system of private law that relied on voluntary organizations, privately administered civil penalties, and restitution rather than punishment for transgressions, that was apparently quite successful. When the English realized they had no "king" or grand monarchy, they declared them barbarians and were able to invade and destroy the system.

Modern Switzerland and Liechtenstein. In Switzerland, the central government is so weak that most citizens don't know the president's name. Power is concentrated in the localities, followed by the cantons and the central government. If one town becomes overbearing, people can and do vote with their feet. Liechtenstein is probably the most libertarian country on this earth currently; each town has the constitutional right to secede from the country if they feel the central government is too overbearing. As many services as possible are provisioned privately and at the local level.

The area of Moresnet (near Belgium) in the 19th century. This little sliver of land was left alone by all nation states for a century, and the people there governed themselves privately and non-coercively without a government. They did all the things such as administer justice and maintain roads, which are supposedly "impossible" without a government.

There are others, but if you are interested, these form a good starting point for further exploration.

To continue to explore this idea, read:
Peter C Earle, *A Century of Anarchy*
Murray Rothbard, *For a New Liberty*
Murray Rothbard, *Conceived in Liberty*
Prince Hans-Adam II of Liechtenstein, *The State in the Third Millennium*
Finbar Feehan-Fitzgerald, *Private Law in the Emerald Isle* (online article)

29

How would X work in a libertarian society?

So how would things work in a truly libertarian society? How would people live together if they were totally free of coercion?

Honestly, nobody knows. It's like asking the Wright brothers to design an F15, or asking Alexander Graham Bell what frequencies cell phone towers should use, or asking a Sumerian banker what the risk profile of mortgage-backed securities would be in an inflationary environment. Even though these people were geniuses that made huge advances, there is so much hard work, innovation and invention between their discovery and where we are now that they could not have foreseen (or even understood) the problem, much less the solution.

When thinking about liberty, we have some examples of societies that were more rooted in liberty than power, and there have been a lot of great thinkers who have tried to figure out how a society without institutionalized aggression might work and have proposed various solutions. So we have some starting points for organizing a free society. But as the shortcomings of these solutions emerge, we would expect more brilliant entrepreneurs to come up with brilliant solutions to problems that we can't even foresee at this moment. There's not a perfect, finished blueprint for a "libertarian society"; we would expect its institutions to change and evolve.

Over the last decades, one of the fastest evolving areas of society has been the technology and software sector. Capabilities exist now that weren't even a pipe dream 20 years ago. The progress has been truly remarkable. One of the reasons (and there are others) is that the sector was relatively free of regulation and government interference, so innovators were free to try crazy ideas, fail, and try again, without first getting a permit or worrying about their license being taken away because they strayed from the approved practices. Imagine if the brilliance, innovation and progress we've seen in software and technology could be applied to education, healthcare and governance. Who could even imagine what society might look like in 50 years?

A totally free society would not necessarily be a society where all problems are solved and all suffering is eliminated. Neither libertarians, nor anyone else, should ever make this claim. Libertarianism should be, if nothing else, eminently practical. Human beings are not going to change any time soon. They will still have tendencies to be greedy, self-centered and lazy. There will still be criminals, cads and thugs. Humans are not perfect and therefore no human society is perfect. There is no utopia. But in a free society there will also be visionaries, philanthropists geniuses and innovators that will continue to apply human ingenuity to solving ever more of our problems, and finding better institutions to channel human action into productive and moral ends.

Also, getting to a totally free society would have to be a long journey. The muscles of liberty in the people are weak and need some exercise before they would be ready for the journey. As an example, there would be no mandatory, government-run Social Security program in a free society since the involuntary confiscation of people's money – taxation — is aggression. That does not mean that we should end Social Security benefits tomorrow. Since the program was started, many people have grown up with the idea that the government will provide for them in retirement, and thus have neglected to adequately prepare for retirement. Cutting off Social Security pensions abruptly would be cruel and unfair. Nevertheless, the vision of a free society shows the direction to go in — somewhere along this journey, we'd have to find a compassionate way to end this program (and many others), and replace it with something voluntary.

30

How would law work in a society free of institutionalized aggression?

This is a variation on "how would X work?" but deserves special mention because it is one of the most thorny issues. As we discussed, there *must* be law in society. There will *always* be those who want to get ahead by hurting others, taking their stuff, or lying and committing fraud. *Someone* needs to enforce the laws when this happens. And this someone needs to have power, and be empowered to use force against criminals. But the danger is that this very someone who is supposed to protect us tends to evolve into someone that oppresses us and destroys the very liberties they are supposed to protect. How to balance these facts is a major challenge for a non-coercive, voluntary society, or in fact, in any society.

For the last millennium or so, it has been government that enforces the laws. The old days in England where private common law judges administered justice are mostly forgotten. The big problem with a supreme authority enforcing law with monopoly power is, of course, that they tend not to enforce it on themselves so much. In the first part of the 21st century, we have seen multiple whistleblowers come forward to expose government employees *breaking the law* and committing wrongdoing. In *every single case*, the *only* person who went to jail was the whistleblower. The people who actually broke the law went free, while the person who did their duty under legal and moral codes was jailed *by the government*. So we need to look for ways to break the government's monopoly on use of force.

Of course, being as inexperienced in liberty as we are, we have trouble imagining how this might work. We don't have the decades or centuries of trial-and-error experience to draw upon. But some thinkers have come up with some schemes that might offer promise.

Think about your car getting stolen. Very often the police will shrug their shoulders, but an insurance investigator might actually find and return the car. The insurance company has *skin in the game* - they have to pay up if the car is not found. The police get paid either way. Incentives make all the difference.

So one idea is that perhaps we would have crime insurance. You would sign up with one of a multitude of providers, and they would insure you against assault, rape, theft, swindling, fraud, etc. Like today's insurance companies, they might charge different rates depending on your lifestyle, thereby discouraging antisocial or dangerous behavior. Insurance companies could hire private security to police the streets or other crime hotspots, because that's a lot cheaper than paying out claims.

Disputes would be handled in private courts or in arbitration. (Already today, very few crimes in the US are tried in the courts — most are handled by plea bargaining and many disputes are handled by professional arbitrators.)

Obviously there are a lot of "what about"s in this discussion. We won't rehash the entire idea here; you can read the article cited below for a good start to this discussion. As you read, please try to remember: 1) that this is really just a guess; we have so few examples to draw on, and 2) the system described will not be perfect, but neither is our current system: people are still murdered and robbed, innocents are executed, millions of non-violent offenders are locked up in cages, etc.

To continue to explore this idea, read:
Hans-Hermann Hoppe, *The Ideas of a Private Law Society* (online article)
Richard Maybury, *Whatever Happened to Justice?*

31

What is restorative justice?

Restorative justice is what you learned in kindergarten - if you break another kid's toy, make it up to him. Our legal system runs on punitive justice - if you break the law, your life can be made miserable.

The punitive system that we live under seems so normal. When you think about it, however, it puts the emphasis on punishing the aggressor, and almost nothing on making the victim whole. For example, if someone steals your car and totals it, the justice system will put that person in jail, but you won't get your car back. And to add insult to injury, you are taxed to keep the perpetrator in jail! So you lose twice. Seeing the crook in jail is supposed to make you feel better, but what if you just want your car back?

Restorative justice focuses on the victim. If someone stole and wrecked your car, they would have to buy you a new one. If the crime was less easily quantifiable, like assault, the case might go to an arbitrator where a sum could be agreed upon. Or the victim might demand other compensation: that the criminal donate time to a community cause, or even write a letter of apology.

If the convict could not pay the agreed-upon fine, they might be sent to a debtors' prison, where they would work, but pay almost all of their salary to the victim until the debt was discharged. Using force to restrict the movements of a convicted criminal would likely be permitted in a libertarian society — many feel that once you have initiated aggression, you have forfeited the protection of the non-aggression principle.

To continue to explore this idea, read:
Mary Ruwart, *Healing Our World*

32

But I *want* to be a socialist!

Then you are in luck! A libertarian society, despite socialism being almost the opposite of libertarianism, is where you want to be!

You see, if you wanted to join a socialist collective, or community, or county, you would be perfectly free to do so, as long as you don't try to shove it down everyone else's throat. As long as the decision to join and leave is voluntary, and not driven by coercion, no one can legally stop you. This applies for any other living arrangement as well. All forms of voluntary association are permitted.

This also means that if your preferred type of community is not viable — Austrian economics can demonstrate that socialism would not be a stable structure, no one is coming to bail you out. High-spending communities would not be bailed out by high-saving communities. So we would learn pretty fast what sorts of living arrangements produce prosperity and which produce poverty.

Currently, evidence shows that free-market capitalism under a system of liberty produces the most peace and prosperity. But who knows if future geniuses might come up with different rules that work even better? In our current one-size-fits-all system, experimentation is incredibly difficult, so we are unlikely to see much innovation in this area until we truly embrace liberty.

33

What's wrong with majority rule?

Many people in modern America assume democracy, and the principle of majority rule, is sacrosanct. But a small amount of thought will show this to be incorrect.

Hitler was elected in a free election, and the majority of Germans, at least in the beginning, supported him. In the US, the majority of people at one time believed in slavery, thought interracial marriage was ungodly, agreed with interning Japanese-Americans, thought gays should not marry, believed women should not vote...and on and on.

Thomas Jefferson said, "A democracy is nothing more than mob rule, where 51 percent of the people may take away the rights of the other 49". The Bill of Rights was in part meant to be a protection of minorities from a majority government.

History has shown again and again that a skillful manipulator can whip a society into a frenzy, and focus their anger on just about any group singled out as a scapegoat. If the majority votes to visit harm on all members of a certain ethnic group, surely that cannot be a moral or legal decision.

The only sure defense here is a fierce adherence to the non-aggression principle, and a refusal to deal with people as groups. If an individual has not committed a violation of that principle, then no one is justified using violence against them.

To continue to explore this idea, read:
Hans-Hermann Hoppe, *Democracy, The God That Failed*

34

You would let people take recreational drugs???

In a word, yes. Libertarians have been fighting for decriminalization of drugs for decades. Don't hurt people, don't take their stuff, don't lie - taking drugs doesn't violate any of these principles.

Note that this does not mean that every libertarian approves of taking recreational drugs - far from it. We just don't support using force to prevent others from taking them.

Also, the War on Drugs, our latest attempt at Prohibition, has been a complete disaster. Millions jailed or killed, entire countries thrown into chaos, crime rates off the charts, all are a result of this misguided war. Close to 80% of US law-enforcement budget is spent on fighting drugs. And guess what? The percent of the population using recreational drugs is pretty much the same as it was 50 years ago, and more people die in the War on Drugs than from drug overdoses.

35

Do libertarians believe in discrimination?

Discrimination is a loaded term in society today, as if it's something inherently bad. Yet we discriminate all the time. "Discrimination" simply means "to differentiate or choose among". We discriminate when we decide who to date or marry, who to hire, and who to hang out with on Saturday night. We make choices like this all the time - without it, life would be kind of meaningless. Imagine that you *had* to date *everyone* that asked - and suitors had to proposition every available candidate - no discrimination allowed!

In a libertarian society, association with other people is voluntary. That also implies that the right to *not* associate is also voluntary. The right to decide to date a certain person means that you are not dating others. Hiring one person means that you are not allowing the others into your company.

Of course we hope that people will discriminate on the basis of other people's character, in accordance with the vision of Martin Luther King. We should look for the most honest, hard-working, loyal, smartest, most adventuresome...whatever it is that is required for the association in question.

Those who judge merely by race, gender, religion, or nationality, when those characteristics have no bearing on the matter at hand, are going to get worse results than those more clear-minded. Over time — no guarantee of quick fixes here — stupid attitudes will die away, if not perpetuated by the government or political entities. But it's safe to say that Jewish bakers would not be forced by men with guns to bake cakes for Nazis.

36

How would libertarians help the unfortunate?

As long as an activity is voluntary and not coerced, it's fine. Government "charity at gun point", where money is taken involuntarily (by force) from you, and spent on programs and recipients where you have no input does not obey the non-aggression principle (don't hurt people, don't take their stuff, don't lie). So libertarians oppose this. Private charity is a whole other thing, and most people, libertarian or not, consider this to be quite noble.

Besides the above moral issue, there is an issue of effectiveness. Consider for example your own family. Who among them "needs help"? Who is down on their luck, who is never going to make it, who is just lazy? How do you help them? Do they need a job? A temporary handout? A loan to start that business they always dreamed about? Do they just need a kick in the pants to get out of their parents' basement? Do they need tough talk? A sympathetic listener? Should you buy groceries for them and take them over every Friday for the rest of your life? Take away their Nintendo?

If you have family members in trouble, you may have already wrestled with these questions. It's not easy, in general, to know how to "help" someone, even if you know them very well.

Now consider a one-size-fits-all government program administered from 2,000 miles away. How in the world are they going to get it right?

A libertarian solution would place the emphasis for helping people first on their family and friends, then on community, church, and charity groups. If the government were to help, primary responsibility should be at the local levels: town or city, followed by county and then state. As propounded in <u>The Wisdom of Crowds</u> by James Surowiecki, people close to the problem have a better chance of solving it, and the more options they have the more creative they can be.

Before the New Deal, individuals organized themselves into "mutual aid associations." These were groups, often united by profession or ethnicity, that insured each other. They paid a membership fee, and the association helped out when they were sick, hurt, or just down on their luck. Help was more carefully tailored because generally the people knew, or at least could meet each other. Arrangements like this are much more efficient and adaptable than large central government programs.

To continue to explore this idea, read:
Joshua Fulton, *Welfare Before the Welfare State* (online article)

About Libertarianism

Mary Ruwart, *Healing Our World*

Economics

Economics deals with money and property. Since libertarian thought deals so much with private property, you might guess that economic thought plays a big role. And you would be right!

Having our stuff taken from us unwillingly - through theft, fraud, inflation, taxes - is a big way in which our liberty is infringed. After all, we invested hours of our precious life on this earth to gain that property. Stealing property is stealing life. Over the centuries, those in power have learned many subtle and sophisticated ways of separating citizens from the wealth they worked to create. We need to understand how economics really works in order to stop the bleeding.

Today is the tomorrow we were told not to worry about by the bad economists of the previous generation. The government borrowed and borrowed, knowing that future generations would have to pay it back. We are future generations.

Let's see if we make the same mistake.

To continue to explore this idea, read:
Henry Hazlitt, *Economics in One Lesson*

37

Why do libertarians talk about economics so much?

Since libertarians love private property, and economics deals with how money and goods flow around the economy, it's no wonder that libertarians love to talk about economics.

It goes beyond that, however. Human beings need stuff to live. We need food, shelter, clothing, and digital televisions. As a reminder, there are two main ways to get what you want - make what you can and trade peacefully and voluntarily for what you want (the economic means) or take what you want by force from someone else (the political means). We've seen previously that one definition of government is the organization of the political means — in blunt terms, it is an organized way of taking wealth from productive people and using it for its own ends. One way that governments do that is through taxation, of course. However, they also manipulate the economy in other ways that transfer wealth to themselves. If you study economics, you can recognize, and oppose, these more subtle attacks on your property.

Imagine that you work for the next 25 years to build a successful career or company, and save up quite a sum of money. How much of that money belongs to me? What is my fair share? How much can I rightfully help myself to the fruits of your labor?

If we are going to advocate for a peaceful and voluntary means of meeting our wants and needs, and reject a force-based approach, then we should take care to understand how a voluntary system works and how best to optimize it. Hence, the study of economics.

In the end, economics is about how people live together, trade, and organize their affairs. It is about how humans act in order to make their lives better. In fact, the masterwork of economist Ludwig von Mises is entitled *Human Action*.

You simply cannot understand how society works without a clear understanding of economics.

To continue to explore this idea, read:
Ludwig von Mises, *Human Action*
Franz Oppenheimer, *The State*

38

Why do libertarians think free trade and capitalism is good?

As we mentioned, there are two ways to get stuff. Find someone who already has stuff, beat the crap out of them, and take it from them. The other is to produce whatever your personal skills make you good at producing, and peacefully and voluntarily trade that with others who have the stuff you want.

If you don't trade, and you reject violence, then you can only have what you can produce yourself. You might be able to paint a ton of houses really well and really fast. But can you get all your own water and food? If you don't trade with farmers, you will die. Maybe you saw the video about the man who tried to build a toaster from scratch. It took him nine months, and still it didn't really work.

It's pretty obvious that the more people you have to trade with, the more you can specialize and the more stuff you can have. If you only traded with people in your town, it's unlikely that you'd have TV sets or cell phones, unless you have all the raw materials, factories, and know-how in your town, *and* those people are not needed to get water from the river or tend crops or cattle.

By trading with larger and larger groups of people, individuals can specialize more. Different groups can figure out how to build cars, and houses, and computers. Some might play sports professionally just to amuse the others. But if your trading is restricted to the nearest three city blocks, you'll be lucky just to have enough to eat.

This system of free trade, otherwise known as capitalism, is one of the most wonderful inventions of the human race. Before its discovery, to get rich you had to beat the daylights out of a lot of people and take their stuff (in other words, you had to be a king or a warlord, or form a government). With the discovery of free-market capitalism, people can focus on producing what their special talents make them good at, and trade *peacefully* for the rest. Besides reducing violence, it has given us a cornucopia of wealth unimaginable by our ancestors.

To continue to explore this idea, read:
Gene Callahan, *Real Economics for Real People*
Thomas Thwaites, *How I Built a Toaster - From Scratch* (online article and video)

39

What's the difference between wealth and money?

This one is so simple, and yet really hard for people to understand, because the two are conflated in the media. Simply put, *wealth* are goods (stuff, like cell phones and cars) and services (like cell phone service, a massage or haircut), whereas *money* is the medium of exchange we use to exchange and trade goods and services. If you have money, you have a claim on goods and services in the future: if you have $20 in your pocket, it's pretty useless, until you go to the corner store and buy some food. The food you can eat *now*; the money just means you can get some food *in the future*.

Imagine if we woke up tomorrow and all the money was gone - no cash, no checks, no credit cards, all the bank accounts were empty. It would be a massive disruption to the economy, but we'd still have houses to live in. Our cars still run. There's still food in the grocery store. But imagine if all the wealth disappeared - we all woke up naked in a field, but everyone had a bag of money - but there was nothing to buy. All the houses, stores, factories, all of it was gone. We'd all be dead in a week.

Where does one get money? It doesn't just appear in your wallet – you need to get money from *other people*. But why would someone give you their money? It could be a gift, but the most common reason is that you provided them with something they wanted: a good or a service that they valued, at that moment, more than the money they gave you. In this sense, money is a kind of "token of appreciation" that certifies to other people that you have done something good for someone, and you have earned a reward! You get to use your tokens to purchase goods and services that other people have produced.

Now you can see that the amount of money in an economy really doesn't matter. We can't counterfeit our way to national prosperity. The Fed could send us each a check for a million dollars tomorrow, but there's still the same amount of beer on the store shelves, still the same amount of oil under the sea. If we all got instantly "rich" that way, all that would change is the prices: they would go up!

To continue to explore this idea, read:
Frederic Bastiat, *What is Money*

40

How does wealth grow — why are we so darn rich?

A lot of people like to talk about poverty. But let's talk about wealth. We live a lifestyle almost inconceivable to a person from 200 years ago. We can video chat with someone on the other side of the world for free, there's so much to eat that a third of the world's population is obese, we have hot running water and millions of entertainment options 24 hours a day. Even the richest kings of the first 200,000 years of human history had nothing like this. Yet even poor people have this today. How did that happen?

To talk about this, we need to define the words **consumer goods** and **capital goods**. Consumer goods are things you want for their own sake - food, cars, houses, haircuts, beer. Capital goods are things that help you get more and better consumer goods. Things like manufacturing equipment, roads, electrical generators, tools. This category also includes knowledge - we learned *how* to generate electricity, *how* to build computers, etc.

The sole reason we are rich — i.e. have an abundance of consumer goods — is that we have built up our capital stock. We spent the last two hundred years building roads, water and sewage systems, an electrical grid, factories, etc., as well as discovering how to generate electricity, manufacture fertilizer, make light bulbs, build nuclear plants. It is this **capital stock** that makes us rich. If you doubt it, just imagine that tomorrow you woke up and all of it was gone — no roads, running water, or power plants. *And*, people had forgotten how to make this stuff — no one has even heard of asphalt, pipes, or electricity. Our living standard would become equivalent to that of the Stone Age instantly.

How did we get all this capital stock? People *invested* time, money, labor, and effort into figuring this stuff out and then building it up. It was pretty tough, and life in the 19th century, although way better than the 15th century, was not not all peaches and cream. But we owe an incalculable debt of gratitude to the people who ground away and invented and built all this great stuff that makes our modern lives possible. And if we don't preserve and improve our capital stock, our standards of living will decrease.

41

Why does it seem like all the wealth in the country is flowing from the poor and middle class to the rich?

Because it is. This is accomplished partially through the mechanism of inflation.

Imagine again a small town with the usual trades: farmers, bakers, tailors, etc. Let's say they use gold for money and the economy is in roughly a steady state (never really true, but let's just assume so).

One day, someone finds a giant chest of gold in his backyard. This is equivalent to creating new money (what follows applies only to this kind of unearned money, not for money earned because you produced goods and services that a lot of people valued). There are several things he can do with it.

Mostly likely would be that he keeps it for himself. Because now he has so much money, he can buy a lot of stuff; he can command more of the town's resources than before. He can buy more cookies and shoes and watermelons, and there are less for everyone else. Clearly he is better off now. As he spends more and more of his money, all the townspeople eventually have a lot more money, and prices will rise. However, he was temporarily able to claim more than his "fair share" of the wealth of the town. This is the lesson: when new unearned money is introduced to an economy, whoever gets to use it first gets the benefit, at the expense of everyone else.

A second way to deal with the money is to split it equally among everyone. This will be a bigger percentage increase for the poor than the people who were already rich, and the poor will get a commensurately larger share of the town's resources - they can buy another fish for dinner, which means one less fish for someone else.

Yet another way to distribute the new money is to just match the money people already have. So if you have 10 gold coins, you will get 100 new coins from the treasure. If you have 5 coins, you get another 50. In this case, the relative wealth of everyone in the community doesn't change. Very rapidly, prices will go up ten times, and then life will continue on as before. (Note that prices will also rise in the first two scenarios, once the new money is out being traded in the economy).

In none of these scenarios is the *town* any richer. There's still the same number of fish, chairs, and barbers as before. The supply of **wealth** - goods and services - has not changed, only the amount of **money** has. Once the money has flooded the economy, prices rise to a new equilibrium (what most people think of as **inflation**).

Now think of our modern economy. The Federal Reserve insists that creating money will stimulate the economy. But when the Fed creates money (say, by quantitative easing, which introduces new money into the money supply), where does it go? Do they hand it out evenly to everyone? Does every citizen get a $10,000 rebate on their income tax? Is there a matching program, the more you have the more you get?

No. The money is handed out to the major banks and the government. In this manner, they can claim more than their fair share of the country's wealth, leaving everyone else a little worse off. Inflation carried out in this manner is a tax, one that can't be avoided, and one that hits the poor the worst.

John Maynard Keynes, the patron saint of modern, mainstream, neo-classical economics, once said: "There is no subtler, no surer means of overturning the existing basis of society than to debauch the currency. The process engages all the hidden forces of economic law on the side of destruction, and does it in a manner which not one man in a million is able to diagnose."

Now you too can diagnose it.

To continue to explore this idea, read:
Richard Maybury, *Whatever Happened to Penny Candy?*
Henry Hazlitt, *Economics in One Lesson*

42

Who is responsible for all this inflation?

The Federal Reserve.

Libertarians have several problems with the Federal Reserve. The first is that it acts as an involuntary distributor of wealth (from the people to the government and banks) through the mechanism of inflation, as we discussed before. This breaks Rule 2 of "Don't hurt people, don't take their stuff, don't lie."

The second is that by essentially allowing the government to print counterfeit money, it enables bad behavior, like wars, to be financed. No modern, major war has been financed out of tax revenue, in any country - the taxpayers would not stand for it. No central banks, no war, no 100-million-plus casualty list.

Another way the Fed takes people's stuff is through bank bailouts. Through the magic of fractional reserve banking, commercial banks create money out of thin air, lend it out, and charge interest on the loans for their trouble. When borrowers get in trouble, they extend more loans, leading to more interest income for the bank. When the borrower finally goes belly up, the US taxpayer bails them out — either through the Fed, World Bank, or IMF — even though the taxpayer never got any of that interest on the loans in the first place.

Yet another problem is that the Fed's interventionism in the money supply causes the boom-bust business cycle. We'll talk about this next.

A money supply that could not be tampered with - either gold-backed, or maybe a cryptocurrency - would go a long way to reigning in the most horrific abuses of power by modern governments. And that's why they will fight it with all their power.

To continue to explore this idea, read:
G. Edward Griffith, *The Creature From Jekyll Island*
Murray Rothbard, *What has the Government Done to Our Money*
Richard Maybury, *Whatever Happened to Penny Candy*

43

Why do booms and busts occur?

Booms occur when the money supply is inflated, making it appear that there are more savings than there actually are, causing people to start projects that should not have been started. The bust comes when it is clear that the resources aren't there, debt and companies are liquidated and the money supply is deflated.

Say what?

Likely, that was as clear as mud. So let's try a simplified example that will make it clear. Remember, money is not wealth. Wealth is real, like physical stuff, labor, and knowledge. Money should serve as a measure of wealth - the more wealth, the more money.

Imagine a small town where everyone is a farmer and grows grain. One day, a bright young person has an idea for how to build an irrigation system that could bring more water to the fields and increase the yields. After mulling it over, the plan is for a group of 10 people to work on this idea for several months to bring it to fruition. Of course, they have to eat during this time, and let's just say they each will need 100 pounds of grain, for a total of 1000 pounds.

Luckily, each farmer keeps their surplus grain in a warehouse in the middle of town. The warehouse is run by a guy they call the banker. Since he's in the middle of town, let's call him the central banker. The banker keeps the grain (wealth) safe in the warehouse, and for every pound he prints a certificate (money) for the depositor, so that he can come back to claim his grain at a later time. When the new water company is started, the people who own the surplus grain lend money to the water entrepreneur, with the understanding that it will be paid back with a little bit of interest, by handing over these certificates, each good for a pound of grain.

Now, if this farming community is not very profitable — profit being the difference between what they produce and what they consume — there might not actually be 1000 pounds of saved grain. If this is the case, the irrigation project will never start, no matter how brilliant it is and no matter how much it would increase yields — the members of the newly formed water company would starve to death before the project was completed.

But let's say that our farmers are a little more productive, and the community has managed to save 3500 pounds of grain. Let's also imagine that three other smart people have equally clever plans to improve the wealth of the community, and that each plan likewise requires 1000 pounds of grain to keep the team alive long enough to finish the project and get the benefits.

Clearly, only three of the projects should be started, because that's all the savings that are available. "Hmm," says the central banker, "surely four new companies would be better than three. It would create 10 more new jobs. I think I'd better stimulate the economy." Our sneaky little banker recalibrates the scale so that the saved 3500 pounds of grain actually reads 4500 pounds. Mind you, there's no new grain, but he prints a thousand new certificates saying that there is. The money supply has been inflated.

What's going to happen here? As the four new companies work on their projects, they'll be consuming the savings in the bank. Eventually, it's going to be clear that there's not enough grain left to feed all 40 people until the end of each project. At this point, people might start bidding more than one certificate for a pound of grain, resulting in price inflation. Eventually, however, someone is going to have to "go bust" and shut down their company, and fire everyone. The longer it takes to realize the trick that the central banker played, the worse the fallout will be. If he hides the grain stores, everyone will be happily working until the last bit of savings is used up, at which point he can no longer redeem certificates with grain. Then all four companies would immediately need to shut down, everyone would have to go back to farming, and a recession would ensue. What's worse, the community's store of savings is gone now and they won't be able to re-attempt the irrigation project until they've saved more grain. The loans taken out by our entrepreneurs are either liquidated, or they are shackled with debt for a long time and can't take on any more projects until they repay it.

New projects and companies, no matter how wonderful, need to be funded out of *savings* (the excess of what is *produced* over what is *consumed* - otherwise known as *profit*). When the money supply is *inflated*, making it seem like there are more savings than there actually are, a *boom* starts and *malinvestment* occurs. Eventually it is realized that there's too much froth in the economy, the central bank decreases the money supply (*deflation*) to stave off rapid price inflation, and the excess projects must be wound down, causing a *recession*.

This basically is Austrian Business Cycle Theory. Grain refers to goods and services produced in the economy, farming refers to productive work, and the certificates represent money. In a huge and complex economy like our own, with lots of savings, these shenanigans can go on for a long time. In a smaller system, like our little town, the consequences could be lethal.

Note also that if the irrigation project had succeeded, and brought water to the village, the farmers' yields would have been increased. Let's say a farmer used to grow 50 pounds a month, but with the new water supply, he can grow 70 pounds a month. If he pays the water company 10 pounds a month, he is still better off, and the water company can use that "money" to pay off the debts they started with. The water company will of course have ongoing maintenance and costs. If the 10 pounds per farmer per month (*revenue*) exceeds their *costs* (in other words, if they are *profitable*), they can pay back their loans *and* the community will soon have an even larger pool of savings with which to start new projects. Everybody wins. If the water company operates at a loss, again, soon the pool of savings will be consumed, they will have to shut down operations, and the community loses all their savings. Everyone loses.

This is why you hear people saying that earning *profit* is the most moral thing you can do. Operating at a loss could kill everyone!

44

How is crony capitalism different from free-market capitalism?

In a free-market system, companies are free to sell what consumers want and consumers are allowed to buy it or not, as they see fit. The only way to get rich is to produce more of what consumers want, or to do it better, or both — like Apple did in the early 21st century. If coercion is forbidden, you need to lure customers with your services and products - if you don't make the people happy, they'll take their dollars elsewhere. Consumers vote with their wallet.

However, this is really hard. Staying on top of fickle consumer sentiment is difficult, and requires constant effort. Savvy competitors constantly spring up and try to eat your lunch. Large companies have come and gone this way (think Kodak, Palm Pilot, Blockbuster, etc). What the company needs is some help - some muscle to keep customers paying and keep competitors out. Of course, that would be illegal for a company to do. Enter the government.

When the government starts deeply regulating an industry, with all sorts of compliance and safety regulations, it presents an irresistible opportunity for companies. Why spend millions on uncertain marketing initiatives and new product development when you can drop five or six figures on a politician and get some predictable and favorable regulation backed by government force? And the enforcement is paid for by the taxpayers (consumers) themselves! The return on investment is huge.

This marks the advent of *crony* capitalism, where one of the main weapons used by corporations for getting rich is the government and the regulatory structure. From taxi companies lobbying for a complete ban of Uber, to large banks purchasing regulatory regimes so burdensome that smaller, nimbler competitors simply go broke, crony capitalism changes the winners from the companies that the consumers love the most to the companies that have purchased the most effective politicians and regulators. Consumers become secondary.

When you think about companies that are hated by consumers, take a look for the involvement of government. Are there thickets of regulations to keep competitors at bay? Are the companies breaking the rules, but somehow shielded from prosecution by the government? Generally this is the case. In areas where there is little government involvement, like online services, creativity flourishes and competition is fierce.

Daniel Hannan was a Member of the European Parliament for the UK for 17 years. He stated that before he went to Brussels, he thought he would be in a struggle to impose regulations on multinational corporations, who would fight back for deregulation. Instead, he found the exact opposite — multinational corporations were *bringing legislation to him* to enact regulations on their own industries. He soon realized that the reason was they were building a regulatory moat around their franchise to prevent upstart competitors from gaining a foothold. Once that moat is complete, the fleecing of the consumer can begin.

Scholars that study regulation state that most regulations have the effect of protecting corporations from competition and from their customers.

To continue to explore this idea, read:
Henry Hazlitt, *Economics in One Lesson*
Hunter Lewis, *Economics in Three Lessons*
Roderick T. Long, *Corporations Versus the Market* (online article)

45

Why are monopolies bad?

The magic of the marketplace occurs through voluntarism — there are multiple providers for everything. If you don't like the service of one, you can use another. This competition to make consumers happy is what pushes progress forward, and eliminates bad actors from the market. Most companies, in particular companies in competitive markets, are terrified of a bad review on social media, and worry about the damage a single unhappy customer can cause, so much so that they fall over backwards trying to make people happy.

Now think of the monopolies in your life - goods and services that are only provided by one provider. Don't we just love our cable companies, the DMV, the public schools, the police, the post office... It's not to say that these organizations *can't* provide high quality and low prices, but all the incentives are stacked against them. As soon as customers *can't* leave, focus shifts to internal politics and bureaucracy sets in, and the company starts telling the consumers what they can and cannot do - the exact opposite of a free market.

One thing to note: most monopolies are created, regulated, and protected by the government. In fact, many economic scholars have stated that there has never been a natural, long-term monopoly, that in fact all monopolies are government-created.

This is the big problem with government: they have a *monopoly* on force and decision-making authority, even in matters concerning themselves. They determine their own income and decide what services to offer and how, and at what price. There's not a shred of please-the-customer thinking in there.

Many libertarian thinkers have theorized how we might have a *selection* of governments — if you don't like government A, switch to government B. Find the one that gives the best service (in your opinion) for the lowest cost. That would keep government bounded.

Not surprisingly, governments absolutely *hate* this idea. In the area of revenue, they call it "tax competition", cast it as a terrible crime, and they form cartels with other governments to keep taxes high. They will not countenance even a small loss of omnipotent authority — for them, every decision ceded back to the individual is a lamentable slide toward their loss of power.

To continue to explore this idea, read:
Murray Rothbard, *For a New Liberty*

46

How can you expect people's needs to be met if you leave it up to the private sector? Somebody needs to plan this out!

Actually, it works much better if no one plans it. Everyone just does what they think is in their interest - change jobs, buy a new car, sell that old lawn mower.

A central planner could not possibly know enough to plan the economy for everyone. We all know everyone is different. Some people are completely risk-averse, whereas others are happy-go-lucky. Some people want lots of money, others value friends more. Some like the city, some like the country. Some save a lot for retirement, others can't abide a life of scrimping and saving, and would rather live for the moment, and the devil may care. Not to mention that there are untold millions of products and services. How in the world would you plan for all of this? In the manner that is called the wisdom of crowds, it's best to let everyone work it out for themselves.

All the individual people, following simple rules ("I make what other people value and will pay for, and use that money to get what I want."), interact to form an incredibly complex dance called the spontaneous order.

To continue to explore this idea, read:
Friedrich Hayek, *The Road to Serfdom*
Friedrich Hayek, *The Use of Knowledge in Society*
Nassim Taleb, *Antifragile*

47

What is the spontaneous order?

Scientists study *complexity science*, with obtuse areas like *emergent behavior* and *self-organized criticality*. One of the key insights from this study is that large systems, with very simple rules can exhibit incredibly complex and ordered behavior. A favorite example is a flock of birds or a school of fish. There's no lead fish with a megaphone shouting "Everyone turn left NOW!" Each individual fish or bird follows a very simple set of rules, but the effect of having many of them together creates elaborate and complex patterns.

The same thing happens in the economy. Each individual actor, following simple rules (don't waste money, try to earn profit, etc.) acts locally without direction, but the end result is a beautiful and complex system that no single mind, or committee of the wise, could possibly have conceived.

This is pointed out in the classic *I, Pencil*. This tiny little monograph points out that the effort of tens of thousands of people must be coordinated and synthesized just to produce a lowly pencil. And yet there always seem to be pencils, everywhere in the world, and in just about the right quantity too — not to mention crazy cheap. Surely there must be a Pencil Czar somewhere, directing and coordinating all these actors, to achieve such a sublime result. In fact, there is no one human being who knows how to create a pencil — the amount of knowledge and range of skills exceeds the capacity of any one person or committee.

So how do these pencils all get made? The market **self-organizes**, and a **spontaneous order** arises, where all the tens of thousands of people do exactly the right thing at exactly the right time in exactly the right quantity *with no central authority to guide them*!

Ok, so surely they must have very dense communications - school teachers are calling up the graphite miners and the yellow paint manufacturers, and telling them how many pencils they will need next year, right? Far from it. The medium of communication are the *prices* of the raw materials and intermediate products. Producers create as much wood, paint, graphite, and little rubber erasers as they can at a profitable price — a price set by the free market. It is this price mechanism, an impersonal set of numbers ("graphite, $10 a ton!") that coordinates the entire system. If there are alternate uses for graphite that consumers prefer, the price is bid up, signalling that more graphite should be diverted to the alternate use. The price of pencils goes up and people buy fewer of them. It's breathtakingly elegant and beautiful.

That's why attempts to interfere with prices - price controls, tariffs, minimum wages - reduce the efficiency of the market and we get less of what we need, or at the wrong time or place, or it's simply more expensive.

To continue to explore this idea, read:
Leonard Reed, *I, Pencil*
FaithWorkEcon, *I, Smartphone* (online video)
Ludwig von Mises, *Human Action*
Murray Rothbard, *Man, Economy, and State*
Hunter Lewis, *Economics in Three Lessons*
M. Mitchell Waldrop, *Complexity: The Emerging Science at the Edge of Order and Chaos*

48

But I want a guaranteed income!

There are no guarantees in life. *No* guarantees. The *only* way to guarantee anything is to use violence to force others to guarantee it for you. This is not acceptable in a libertarian philosophy.

Even guarantees obtained through force cannot be counted on. Right now in Venezuela, the entire economy is grinding to a halt as the country goes bankrupt after 15 years of socialist economic policy. Government social programs and transfer payments have stopped. Middle-class professionals are searching garbage cans for food to eat. So much for their government guarantees. No such deprivation has been reported among top-level government officials.

49

What are essential differences between socialism and free-market economics?

This is a very large subject, but here's a little mental model that might help you think about this area. We already know that humans use division of labor to become more efficient. Think of all the people in the economy, producing goods and services: popsicles, furniture, health care, solar panels, etc. Imagine that they put all of these goods and services into a big pile in the middle of a field. This is the output of the economy. We produce in order to consume, of course, so now the question becomes: how do we divvy up all this wonderful loot?

Socialism and other forms of collectivism might advocate distributing this wealth "to each according to his need." This sounds humane, but a big problem lurks: how to assess someone's need? The assessment needs to be precise and quantitative, because we have a quantitatively precise pile of goods and services to divvy up. Of course, there is no objective way to do this, so committees are set up to assess everyone's "need" and supply them with wealth accordingly.

Do you see the horrific flaw in this plan? Remember, everyone wants to get ahead, everyone wants to better their situation, everyone wants more. In this scheme, the division of wealth is entirely political – subjective judgements of a small group of individuals. The way to get ahead now is to play politics: if I can just convince the committee that we are in more need, I can get more stuff. On the other hand, if I have a disagreement with anyone on the committee, I might find my "need" downsized, along with my house and car. Political maneuvering and skill would be essential for survival. Those running the committees have essentially the power of life and death over those whose need they are evaluating. Power like this will corrupt anyone's soul (see, for example, the Stanford Prison Experiment). The evil a scheme like this would unleash is unimaginable.

Another method might be to divide things equally. This plan shares an additional flaw exhibited by the "need" scheme above. There is no incentive to work harder or smarter or to have great ideas or to invent smart phones or anything in this scheme. Increasing (or decreasing) your efforts has essentially zero impact on your outcomes. As psychological research has shown, when outcomes are unaffected by efforts, organisms (animals as well as people) tend to fall into deep depression and cease striving. When no matter what you do, the outcome is the same, you lose the will to live. Your efforts, your passion, your genius, your hard work is completely irrelevant. What an awful way to live.

One of the few ways, perhaps the only way, to provide a way to divvy up the pile without destroying the spirit of those contributing is to let everyone take out an amount equal to what they put in. In that way, everyone is incentivized to put as much in as they can. The way to get ahead is clear: make more things that people want, and add them to the pile. The pile gets bigger and bigger, and everyone feels a sense of accomplishment and feels in control of their lives.

This little metaphor only extends so far, and of course the real economy doesn't work quite like this (we don't put our stuff into a big pile, we exchange one-to-one, and one person's invention might make many others more efficient, etc.), but it does provide a simple framework for thinking about some of these issues.

50

What is Austrian economics?

Austrian economics is the perspective used in this chapter to explain economic concepts. The school of economics that has its roots, not surprisingly, in Austria. But contributors to this school of thought have come from all over the globe.

Whereas neo-classical, mainstream economics tends to look at aggregate measures (like GDP, unemployment, etc.) and considers humans to be little interchangeable rational decision-making machines, the Austrian school treats economics more as an observational science and puts humans in the center. Why do people live like they do? Why do they spend their time and money as they do? How do they cooperate with each other to get what they want?

Here's a small parable that might make the differences more clear. Suppose there are two cities: one is up in the foothills of the mountains, in a beautiful spot, clean and quiet. There's not a lot of industry there, and so incomes are rather low. Another town, down in the valley, is bursting with industriousness. Incomes are high, but the city is noisy and dirty, and everyone works very hard. Which people are better off?

Mainstream economics would look at the higher salaries and conclude the valley town is definitely better off. Their per capita income is much higher and therefore they are much richer and better off. In fact, mainstream economics might recommend that the mountain city try to attract industry like the valley did. Not doing so is considered irrational, a failing to be corrected. They might even recommend that the government create policies to basically force people to move from the mountain to the valley, so that they can be "better off".

The Austrians would look at this situation and assume that the residents of the mountain city are there because they *like* it. After all, if they thought they would be better off in the valley, they would move there. Maybe they value the clean, cool air more than they value a higher income. Maybe they like the close-knit culture. An Austrian economist would assume that any outside force, i.e. government, that intervened to change the situation would actually be making things worse. In Austrian economics, "aggregate GDP" is not necessarily an indicator of being better off.

Mainstream economics spends a lot of time trying to explain why people are "irrational" — they assume that everyone would make every decision based on the cash value of the results, and when they don't, economists talk about changing their behavior. For example, some people save a lot of money for retirement; others don't. Perhaps the thought of a life scrimping and saving in order to make their golden years comfortable is not an attractive thought. For a mainstream economist, this is an irrationality to correct; for an Austrian, it is a preference to understand.

Austrians also talk about *revealed preference*. Marketers will get this immediately: if you ask people, "Would you buy this widget for $20?", they might overwhelmingly say yes, but once you ask for the cash, suddenly far fewer are interested. What people *say* they want or would do is not that interesting; what they *actually* do when they have to fork over the cash or spend the time is what is interesting to economists (and marketers).

If the topic of economics has always been confusing and arcane to you, try looking into Austrian economics. It deals with the real choices of real people and the basic concepts will be completely accessible for you.

To continue to explore this idea, read:
Gene Callahan, *Real Economics for Real People*

Summary

I hope I've been able to convey to you that libertarianism is a philosophy of – actually *the* philosophy of – peaceful coexistence, of how we can live together in society without violence. It's not a right-wing philosophy, nor is it a left-wing philosophy. Libertarianism celebrates diversity – not the trivial kind of skin color and nose shape, but the diversity of talents, preferences, opinions, capabilities, and skills that are the glory of the human race. Living without aggression allows each individual the opportunity to grow to their greatest potential.

Although some conclusions of libertarian thought might be startling at first glance, I hope by now you realize that there is a deeply reasoned and principled structure of thought underlying those conclusions, backed by logic and scholarly research.

The key insight of libertarianism is that the non-aggression principal – don't hurt people, don't take their stuff, don't lie – is the fundamental moral principal that binds all human beings' interactions with other human beings. No one gets a free pass on this, including and especially people who work for the government. To have a truly free society, everyone must be on board.

I wish you all peace, and a life free from violence!

www.ingramcontent.com/pod-product-compliance
Lightning Source LLC
Chambersburg PA
CBHW070127260726
48658CB00001B/293